Chris Webber

Additional Titles in the Sports Reports Series

Andre Agassi
Star Tennis Player
(0-89490-798-0)

Troy Aikman
Star Quarterback
(0-89490-927-4)

Roberto Alomar
Star Second Baseman
(0-7660-1079-1)

Charles Barkley
Star Forward
(0-89490-655-0)

Terrell Davis
Star Running Back
(07660-1331-6)

Tim Duncan
Star Forward
(0-7660-1334-0)

Dale Earnhardt
Star Race Car Driver
(0-7660-1335-9)

Jeff Gordon
Star Race Car Driver
(0-7660-1083-X)

Wayne Gretzky
Star Center
(0-89490-930-4)

Ken Griffey, Jr.
Star Outfielder
(0-89490-802-2)

Scott Hamilton
Star Figure Skater
(0-7660-1236-0)

Anfernee Hardaway
Star Guard
(0-7660-1234-4)

Grant Hill
Star Forward
(0-7660-1078-3)

Michael Jordan
Star Guard
(0-89490-482-5)

Shawn Kemp
Star Forward
(0-89490-929-0)

Jason Kidd
Star Guard
(0-7660-1333-2)

Mario Lemieux
Star Center
(0-89490-932-0)

Karl Malone
Star Forward
(0-89490-931-2)

Dan Marino
Star Quarterback
(0-89490-933-9)

Mark McGwire
Star Home Run Hitter
(0-7660-1329-4)

Mark Messier
Star Center
(0-89490-801-4)

Reggie Miller
Star Guard
(0-7660-1082-1)

Chris Mullin
Star Forward
(0-89490-486-8)

Hakeem Olajuwon
Star Center
(0-89490-803-0)

Shaquille O'Neal
Star Center
(0-89490-656-9)

Gary Payton
Star Guard
(0-7660-1330-8)

Scottie Pippen
Star Forward
(0-7660-1080-5)

Jerry Rice
Star Wide Receiver
(0-89490-928-2)

Cal Ripken, Jr.
Star Shortstop
(0-89490-485-X)

David Robinson
Star Center
(0-89490-483-3)

Barry Sanders
Star Running Back
(0-89490-484-1)

Deion Sanders
Star Athlete
(0-89490-652-6)

Junior Seau
Star Linebacker
(0-89490-800-6)

Emmitt Smith
Star Running Back
(0-89490-653-4)

Frank Thomas
Star First Baseman
(0-89490-659-3)

Thurman Thomas
Star Running Back
(0-89490-445-0)

Chris Webber
Star Forward
(0-89490-799-9)

Tiger Woods
Star Golfer
(0-7660-1081-3)

Steve Young
Star Quarterback
(0-89490-654-2)

SPORTS REPORTS

Chris Webber

Star Forward

Ron Knapp

Enslow Publishers, Inc.

40 Industrial Road   PO Box 38
Box 398   Aldershot
Berkeley Heights, NJ 07922   Hants GU12 6BP
USA   UK

http://www.enslow.com

Library of Congress Cataloging-in-Publication Data

Knapp, Ron.
     Chris Webber : star forward / Ron Knapp.
        p. cm. —(Sports reports)
     Includes bibliographical references and index.
     Summary: A biography of the young player who was a member of the
University of Michigan's "Fab Five" in 1993 and Rookie of the Year in the NBA
the next year.
     ISBN 0-89490-799-9
     1. Webber, Chris, 1973–   —Juvenile literature. 2. Basketball players—
United States—Biography—Juvenile literature. [1. Webber, Chris, 1973– .
2. Basketball players. 3. Afro-Americans—Biography.] I. Title. II. Series.
GV884.W36K53 1997
796.323'092—dc20
[B]

                96-9133
                  CIP
                  AC

Printed in the United States of America

10 9 8 7 6 5 4 3

To Our Readers:
All Internet addresses in this book were active and appropriate when we went to
press. Any comments or suggestions can be sent by e-mail to Comments@enslow.com
or to the address on the back cover.

Illustration Credits: Mitchell Layton Photography, pp. 9, 12, 19, 21, 25, 27,
32, 35, 40, 44, 48, 51, 55, 58, 63, 71, 73, 75, 82, 87, 90, 93.

Cover Photo: AP/Wide World Photos

Contents

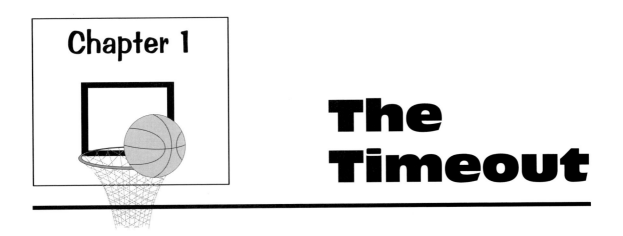

Chapter 1

The Timeout

In 1993, Chris Webber was one of the most famous twenty-year-olds in the United States. His handsome face and shaved head were familiar to millions of college basketball fans.

Teenagers bought thousands of blue Michigan jerseys bearing his bright yellow number. Many of them also wore the same kind of short black socks he pulled over his size 16 feet before the start of every game. Most of all, the kids loved the long, baggy shorts that Chris and his Wolverine team-mates wore low on their hips.

Webber was the best-known member of the Fab Five, Michigan's five great sophomores. When he had enrolled at the university in the fall of 1991 with Ray Jackson, Jimmy King, Jalen Rose, and Juwan

Howard, reporters had called them the greatest group of freshmen ever recruited.

On April 5, the Fab Five were in New Orleans with coach Steve Fisher and the rest of the Wolverines for the championship game of the National Collegiate Athletic Association (NCAA) tournament. It would be their second title game in a row. In 1992, Michigan had been crushed by the Duke Blue Devils, 71–51. In 1993, they would be facing the Tar Heels of North Carolina.

Webber knew that he was a very fortunate young man. "I used to dream about it, but I never thought about it. You know I put myself in those positions, but I never thought it would come to reality. Making it to two Final Fours and two championship games is something I could never fathom. I never thought it would happen. I just dreamed about it."[1]

While he was in New Orleans waiting for the big game, Webber borrowed a piece of jewelry from a teammate to help him dream. It was Rob Pelinka's championship ring, earned when Michigan won the NCAA tournament in 1989. Back then, Chris was still a sophomore in high school.

While he was dreaming, it was impossible to forget what had happened the year before against Duke. "I just know last year losing was the lowest point of my life so hopefully this will be the highest point of my life."[2]

FACT

Steve Fisher became coach of the Michigan basketball team at the start of the 1989 NCAA postseason tournament. The Wolverines took the title when Rumeal Robinson dropped in two free throws with three seconds left in overtime to beat Seton Hall, 80–79, in the final.

Rising high above the competition, Chris Webber moves in for a basket.

As he walked into the Superdome for the title game, Chris had no idea that he was about to have an even worse experience than the Duke game.

Michigan was the most exciting team in college basketball. Led by the starting Fab Five, they were young and wild. They made fancy dunks and surprised their opponents with behind-the-back passes. When they did well, they didn't try to hide their happiness; they smiled and celebrated on the court. Their sneers and trash talk were intended to intimidate their opponents. The baggy shorts, black socks, and bald heads made them instantly recognizable. One of the slogans they liked to yell at each other was "Shock the world!"

Of course, not everybody liked the Wolverines. Some fans thought they were undisciplined, obnoxious show-offs. Sure, they were great athletes, but why couldn't they just stick to basketball? Why did they have to look so different from every other team? Why did they have to try to embarrass their opponents? Those fans complained that Coach Fisher let his players run wild.

Michigan would be facing a very different team in the title game. North Carolina, coached by Dean Smith, was a disciplined, quiet squad that didn't try to look—or act—differently from the teams that fans had been watching for decades.

Two years before, Smith was probably the only college coach in America who hadn't wanted Webber on his team. "I don't know how well you'll fit into the program," he had told him. "You ought to go where you can use your ability."[3] A flashy player like Chris wasn't what the Tar Heels were after.

Instead, they had athletes like Eric Montross, a quiet seven-foot center with a crew cut. Despite their differences in style, Webber and Montross were friends. A few years earlier, they had both attended a basketball camp for high school stars at Princeton University. "Eric's a great guy," Chris said.[4]

Most observers agreed that, as individuals, the Wolverines were a far more talented team. If the Tar Heels were to win, they would have to work together very patiently and efficiently. They couldn't lose their composure or try to make a lot of flashy one-man plays, but if each man did his job, Smith was confident his team could win.

Coach Fisher was just as confident. "This is the smartest group of players I've ever been associated with. Obviously, this is also the most talented. But you can't win with one without the other."[5]

Webber looked subdued during introductions as he jogged onto the court, trading high fives with his teammates. A plain blue T-shirt covered his jersey.

FACT

In March, at the end of each college basketball season, sixty-four teams qualify for participation in the single-elimination NCAA tournament. To get to the final championship game, each team must win five games.

Webber celebrates with Bullets' teammate Kenny Walker. While at the University of Michigan, Webber was the leader of the Fab Five.

The leader of the Fab Five wasn't trying to impress anybody with his attitude or his style. He and his teammates were ready to play serious basketball.

Then, Chris missed his first shot, a three-point attempt that clunked off the side of the rim. Montross was hot early, picking up a layup and three free throws. The game seemed to be slipping slowly away from the Wolverines until Webber got past Montross and crashed a dunk. Then it was time for trash talk. "Get used to that. I'm here all night."[6]

Montross wasn't the only Tar Heel giving Michigan trouble, though. George Lynch was tough underneath, grabbing rebounds and blocking shots. Donald Williams was dropping in three-pointers. With forty-nine seconds left in the half, he sunk a long shot to put North Carolina ahead, 42–36.

In the 1992 title game against Duke, the Wolverines had collapsed in the second half, but Webber wasn't about to let that happen against the Tar Heels. In the opening minutes after intermission, he was a hurricane of energy, dashing around the court, making baskets, grabbing rebounds, and blocking shots.

When Rose and King had trouble guarding Williams, Chris helped them out. On one play, Williams didn't notice Webber sneaking up behind him until it was too late. Chris reached over the shorter man's head, tapped the ball away, then grabbed it and headed for the basket.

Nobody could stop him! Slam dunk! The Wolverines were within one, 53–52.

Webber began eating up the Tar Heels under the basket. They couldn't stop his shots or prevent him from grabbing rebounds. With just over four minutes left, Michigan led, 67–63.

Coach Smith knew his team had to change tactics, so he switched the Tar Heels to a zone defense. That move kept Chris from getting the ball under the basket. "When we went to the zone," said Williams, "they got impatient. They wanted to get the ball inside to Webber. They weren't getting good looks at the basket. They wanted to rush their shots."[7]

Another three-pointer by Williams cut the Wolverine lead to 67–66. King tried one of his own, but it bounced off the rim. When he got the ball again, he drove for the basket, but missed again. North Carolina got the ball, and Derrick Phelps dropped in a shot to put his team ahead, 68–67.

King tried another three-pointer, but the ball didn't even reach the rim. He was tired; so was the rest of the Fab Five. They had been on the court for most of the game. Meanwhile, Smith kept shuffling his players. "I think we wore them down a lot," Montross said. "We kept sending players at them."[8]

A Lynch jump shot made it 70–67. When Rose dribbled the ball away, Montross was there for the pass and the dunk. North Carolina led, 72–67. They were a minute away from the national title. In the stands, their fans already began to celebrate.

Jackson took the inbounds pass and quieted the Tar Heel fans with an eighteen-footer for the Wolverines. They trailed by three, 72–69. With forty-eight seconds left, they were a three-pointer away from a tie.

Fisher called a time-out and told his players to press. If they couldn't get the ball back quickly, they would have to foul. Before sending them back to the court, he reminded them that they had no more time-outs left.

As he took the inbounds pass, Brian Reese, of the Tar Heels, stepped on the out-of-bounds line. It was an incredible mistake, the type of error a kid makes in his first junior high game, not in the national championship. Michigan got the ball.

A three-pointer would tie the game, and that's what Rose tried, but it bounced away. Webber attacked the backboard with his long arms, grabbed the ball and laid it in. The Wolverines were down by one, 72–71.

With twenty seconds to go, Pelinka fouled North Carolina's Pat Sullivan. If he missed the first try of a one-and-one situation, the Wolverines could grab the rebound and head downcourt for what they hoped would be a winning basket. If he made the first and missed the second, they could still rebound and be in position for a tying field goal or a winning three-pointer.

"This is for the national championship, baby," Pelinka told Sullivan, as he prepared to shoot.[9] The first shot was good, making it 73–71, but the second bounced off the rim right to Webber.

As the other players raced downcourt, Chris looked toward the basket, then dragged his foot before dribbling. Traveling! The Tar Heels jumped to their feet, yelling. Chris had walked with the ball, a mistake just as bad as Reese's. The referees should have blown their whistles and given the ball to North Carolina.

There were no whistles though, and Michigan kept the ball. Smith and his assistants screamed in protest as Webber dribbled down the right side of the court. Phelps and Lynch didn't bother screaming. As Chris closed in on the basket, they closed in on him.

Pelinka was open. Howard waved his arms, expecting a pass. Chris ignored them both, as he headed for the corner. When he got there, his men were covered, and he couldn't shoot himself. Phelps and Lynch were all over him.

Time was running out. Chris had to do something.

The Michigan bench was trying to tell him what to do. Webber and Lynch both thought they were yelling, "Call time-out! Call time-out!"[10]

So Chris made a T with his hands and called a time-out.

The Tar Heel bench went wild. They remembered something Chris had forgotten: Michigan didn't have any time-outs left. The players on the bench hadn't been yelling, "Call time-out!" They had been telling him, "No time-out!"

Instead of getting time to plan for a last shot, Michigan was socked with a technical foul. Chris had made an incredible mistake. Instead of putting up a possible tying shot, the Wolverines would have to watch Williams make a pair of free throws. It was all over. The Tar Heels were up by four. In the last seconds, Williams sank two more free throws to make the final margin 77–71.

As the buzzer sounded, Chris lowered his head and walked off the court. He couldn't believe what he had done. He felt as if he had personally blown the national championship. How could he have forgotten they were out of time-outs?

"I don't remember," he said quietly. "Just called a time-out, and we didn't have a time-out. And I cost our team the game."[11]

Fisher rushed to defend his young star. "In the heat of the moment strange things happen," he told the millions watching on television. "It's an awful way to have the season end when you've got a chance to get a shot to tie, and no one feels worse than Chris." He wanted people to remember Webber's incredible season and the fine game he had played before making his critical mistake. "We're not here if it's not for Chris."[12]

Pelinka agreed. "Chris is the heart and soul of this team, and he should not be blamed for our loss."[13]

Even Montross came to his friend's defense. In the midst of the Tar Heel celebration, he said, "Don't blame Chris Webber. Blame the coaches. They all should have known better."[14]

Chris never tried to shift the blame onto the Michigan coaching staff, though. He was the one who had made the mistake. He never bothered to point out the big plays he had made against North Carolina, the 23 points he had scored, or his 11 rebounds. Despite what many people were saying, he felt he was the man who had to accept blame for the loss.

After answering all the reporters' questions, Webber showered, dressed, and left the Superdome locker room. With his head down, he walked quietly down a hallway. When a child asked for an autograph, he stopped just long enough to sign, then moved on.

Then he saw his father. Mayce Webber wrapped his six-foot eight-inch son in his arms. The young man bent over to reach his dad and began to cry.

Juwan Howard was another member of the Fab Five. In 1994, Webber and Howard were reunited as teammates on the Washington Bullets.

Chris Webber would never forget that awful night in the Superdome. A few days later, he joked, "Usually in the basketball season, I'm in the mood for no hair. But now I think I'll grow long hair and a beard and move out to Arizona and live in the desert."[15]

Of course, Chris never gave up basketball to live with cactus plants and coyotes—and he never let his hair grow, either. He still had a lot of basketball games left to play.

Chapter 2

Early Life in Detroit

The men in the Webber family have always been tall. Chris's dad, Mayce, claimed that his great-great-grandfather was over seven feet tall.

Besides being tall, they all seemed to like basketball. When he was little, Chris liked to play against his father. As they made their moves on the backyard court, they pretended to be pro superstars. Chris usually wanted to be Bernard King, the high-scoring forward of the New York Knicks, or Magic Johnson, the man who brought championships to Michigan State and the Los Angeles Lakers.

Even though he was still a little boy, Chris was usually able to make the big plays against the older men. "He always hit some kind of shot to win the game," said Mayce. "Even when things went bad, he found a way to make them right. He's always been that way."[1]

Chris has always been close to his family and very proud of his father. In 1993, he summarized his dad's life for a reporter:

"Born in Mississippi, saw a friend of his lynched, worked on a cotton plantation, his mother died when he was seven, he helped raise five kids, quit school after the sixth grade, moved to Detroit, got married, a good job at GM [General Motors], went back to high school, great speaker, very confident— I can't say enough about him."[2]

Mayce was one of the millions of African Americans who moved to the big industrial cities of the North in the years after World War II. In the Southern states, the good jobs were still closed to everybody except white workers. If a black man wanted to earn a good wage, he had to move north. Some of the most popular destinations were the booming automobile factories of the Midwest. Many of them were clustered around Detroit, the "Motor City."

Mayce Webber got a job at a GM plant that manufactured Cadillac cars. His wife, Doris Webber, worked for the Detroit public schools as a special education teacher for high school students.

Their first child was born on March 1, 1973. He was a big baby, and he had a big name—Mayce Edward Christopher Webber III. Chris, as he was

As a young boy, Chris was good enough to play basketball with older men. His father insists that Webber has always been able to make the big play.

called, had an incredible appetite; he always seemed hungry. Of course, as he kept eating, he kept growing.

When he was just ten months old, he took his first steps. Three months later he was able to catch a ball. By the time he started nursery school, he towered over the other children.

Even when he was little, Chris loved to help his parents. One day his father brought out a can of white paint to touch up a picket fence that ran around their yard. When Mr. Webber left the boy alone for a few moments, Chris looked at the paint and at the bright red family car sitting in the driveway. What that car needed, he decided, was a long white streak down the side. So he picked up the brush and went to work.

When his father finally came back out of the house, Chris was very proud of his work. "Doesn't that car look better now?" he asked.

Of course, Mr. Webber wasn't pleased. "I couldn't believe it," he said. "I wanted to strangle him. But he just smiled."[3]

Chris's efforts were much more appreciated when he took care of his baby sisters and his three little brothers. When his mother was tired, he kept the babies quiet by feeding them peanut butter. He learned to fill bottles and change diapers. It wasn't unusual for all five of the younger children to fall asleep at night in the same crowded bed. When it stormed, Chris gathered them together on a blanket in the living room.

Mayce and Doris Webber were loving but strict parents. They expected their children to behave and to do well in school. Every night there was "quiet time" at the house. For an hour, the children could do nothing except read or think. No talking. No playing. No watching TV. "When I'd get home from school," Chris said, "I'd want to go outside and play. My street must have had fifty kids on it, so everybody would be in the streets playing. But I couldn't play until I cleaned up, and then my mom would make us read for an hour. I didn't like it then, but now I'm glad she made me do it."[4]

Even though both his parents had jobs, Chris and his family did not live in a big fancy house. "We came from a terribly bad neighborhood," he said.[5] Some of the children who lived nearby weren't fortunate enough to have parents like his. The kids stayed out late, didn't worry about school, and sometimes got involved with drugs and gangs. "We kept repeating the same things to him," said Mr. Webber, "warning him about drugs, being with the wrong people, being out too long. We tried to give him a good environment."[6]

Of course, it was also important to have fun. That's why his parents encouraged him to play basketball. Almost everybody was sure that was the perfect sport for Chris. After all, when he was in sixth grade he was already six feet tall—and still growing!

When he was twelve, he signed up to play on a neighborhood Amateur Athletic Union (AAU) team. For his first practice, he showed up in a bright Hawaiian shirt. His teammates couldn't stop laughing. Why, they wondered, would anybody be stupid enough to wear something that silly? They didn't realize that Chris didn't know most players would be wearing jerseys or T-shirts.

The other boys kept laughing when Chris started to play. Even though he was very tall, he seemed shy and awkward. It was almost as if he was afraid of the ball. A tall, thin teammate named Jalen Rose told him, "You've got the sorriest game I've ever seen."[7]

When Chris finally left that first practice, he was crying. He didn't like his teammates, and he hated basketball, but his parents expected him to play. When it was time for practice, he left the house, but he didn't go to the court. He went to a friend's house or wandered the neighborhood. He didn't like sneaking around behind his parents' backs, though, so finally he asked his dad if he could quit the team.

"He told me I was going back," Chris said. "There wasn't a lot of discussion about it. He said a man doesn't run away from difficult situations; he stands firm and conquers them."[8]

So Chris went back to the team. It didn't take him long to realize that he was a pretty good player. Of course, it helped to be tall, but he always had big, sure hands, and he was very quick. His only problem was that he wasn't aggressive enough. If he made a mistake or somebody blocked one of his shots, he got upset. When other players insulted him, it hurt his feelings. He always tried to be careful not to bump into his opponents. If he fouled them, he apologized.

Curtis Harvey was one of the first coaches to work with Chris. He came up with a plan to make Chris a mean, aggressive competitor. "Get this kid," he told one of the toughest players. "Hit him. Talk about his mama. Whatever. Don't let up."[9]

Over the next few weeks, Chris had a miserable time at practices. The abuse made him cry and walk off the court, but he never went home. He knew his dad wouldn't let him quit the team, so he always walked back onto the court. After a while, he tried to ignore the insults. Sometimes he even did some trash talking of his own. Instead of crying about having his shots blocked, he learned to avoid his

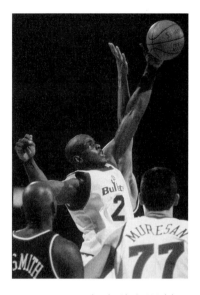

Arms outstretched, Chris Webber tries to pull in the loose ball. Even when he first began playing basketball, it was obvious that Chris had very sure hands.

opponents when he was shooting. He also realized how much fun it was to block their shots.

After a few months, Chris was an excellent player, and he loved the game. Soon he was practicing several hours a day. Harvey organized a team called the Super Friends with Webber, Rose, and other Detroit teenagers. They played at tournaments across the country from Seattle, Washington, to New York City. For two years in a row, Chris was named the most valuable player of the AAU Junior Olympic Games.

When he began enjoying the game, he became good friends with Jalen Rose, the boy who had insulted him at his first practice. Once they were playing with a cap gun. Chris put a big roll of caps in his jeans pocket, and Jalen teased him by putting the toy gun against his pants and firing.

Pop! All the caps in the pocket went off at once.

Jalen was laughing until Chris began to scream. The exploding caps had set his jeans on fire.

Chris was hurting, and he was scared. As he jumped around with his pants burning, he had a terrible time loosening his belt. Finally, Jalen came to his rescue by yanking down the pants and helping his friend stomp out the fire. Four years later, when they both played for Michigan, long baggy shorts hid the scar on Chris's left thigh.

Webber is able to slam-dunk with tremendous force. While playing on a school team, he once made 15 slams in one game.

During the winter months, Chris also played on the Temple Christian School team. In one game, he scored 64 points and made 15 dunks. It wasn't long before he began attracting a lot of attention. When he was still a six-foot-five-inch thirteen-year-old, he was already being interviewed by television reporters.

When Chris told one reporter he wanted to play for Michigan State University someday, he caught the attention of Jud Heathcote, the Spartan coach who had worked with Magic Johnson, Webber's hero. Heathcote invited the boy and his family to come to MSU for a game and a look at the NCAA trophy Johnson's team had won in 1979. The coach hoped that in four years the kid from Detroit would help him win another one.

Of course, before he could enroll in college, Chris had to go to high school. Most people expected him to play for a powerful Detroit public school team, but his mother had other ideas. As a young woman, she had always dreamed of attending Country Day, a private high school in nearby Beverly Hills, Michigan. It had a reputation for requiring a lot of hard work from its students. Since it wasn't a public school, parents were required to pay thousands of dollars in tuition. Doris Webber's parents weren't wealthy, so she hadn't been able to attend. She and her husband weren't rich, either, but because of his grades and his scores on an entrance exam, Chris was eligible for an academic scholarship. That meant his parents wouldn't have to pay the full tuition. Mayce Webber agreed with his wife. "It was very important to us that he have the chance to attend private school."[10]

Kurt Keener had noticed Webber even before the boy began attending classes. He spotted his name on a list of prospective students taking the entrance exam. Keener was Country Day's varsity basketball coach. Like almost every other high school coach in Michigan, he had already heard of Chris Webber. He couldn't wait for basketball practices to begin.

Chapter 3

State Champion

At first Chris Webber didn't like Country Day High School.

The beautiful campus in suburban Beverly Hills was a completely new environment. He had spent his entire life in a lower-middle-class Detroit neighborhood filled with African-American people. Most of the students at Country Day were white, and almost all of them were very rich. "I saw kids get new cars on their sixteenth birthday," he said. "Then I would go home and eat beans for a week."[1]

Country Day students didn't wear jeans and T-shirts. "We had to wear a suit to school every day," Chris said. "I didn't even have a suit."[2] His parents soon made sure that he had the same uniform as every other male student—white shirt, tie, and navy blue blazer with the Country Day insignia on the pocket.

Of course, even with the uniform, Chris didn't look like the other students. He was the only six-foot-five-inch African American on campus. It didn't take him long to decide his new school wasn't for him. "I wanted to go to Southwestern [the big Detroit high school that his friend Jalen Rose attended], but my dad wanted me to go to Country Day to make sure I got an education. He knew I was gonna be OK in basketball."[3]

The ninth grader knew there was no way he could convince his parents to let him switch schools, so he came up with a plan: He would flunk tests on purpose and not do any homework. Soon his grades would be so poor that he would lose his scholarship and get kicked out of Country Day. The scheme didn't work, because Mr. and Mrs. Webber knew Chris was smart enough to pass his classes. They told him to get to work and get serious about his studies. Chris had to resign himself to four years at Country Day.

Not surprisingly, the best part of school was being on the basketball team. Soon he was working out with Coach Kurt Keener and the rest of the Yellowjackets. It seemed strange to be playing on teams made up almost entirely of white players, who weren't nearly as good as Jalen and his other former AAU teammates from Detroit. During

FACT

When Chris Webber was in high school, the Detroit Pistons were known as the "Bad Boys" of the NBA. Isiah Thomas, Joe Dumars, and Dennis Rodman were three stars on the team that took the 1989 and 1990 league titles.

Webber made Michigan's All-State team as a high school freshman.

summer vacations, the games with his old friends were a lot tougher—and a lot more fun. Sometimes Isiah Thomas and other pro players from the Detroit Pistons joined in the action.

Country Day was a small school, so most of the Yellowjackets' games were against teams from other small schools. Southwestern and other powerhouse schools weren't on their schedule. That didn't mean that Webber wasn't noticed. Even as a freshman, he was named to the All-State team by Michigan sportswriters and broadcasters.

In Michigan, all high school basketball teams play in postseason single-elimination tournaments. Fans love the excitement of what they call March Madness. The teams that make it all the way through the tournaments without losing are crowned the state champions. In 1989, when Chris was a sophomore, Country Day was in Class C with dozens of other small schools. Southwestern, was in Class A, of course. While the competition was still going on, Webber was again named to the All-State team. During the 1988–89 season, he had averaged 25 points, 12 rebounds, and 5.7 blocked shots a game.

In the quarterfinals of the postseason tournament, the Yellowjackets demolished Deckerville, 75–37. Then Chris had 25 points and 11 rebounds as Cassopolis fell, 75–53.

The championship games in 1989 were played in Ann Arbor at the University of Michigan's Crisler Arena, a place that would become very familiar to Webber in the years to come. The team from Ishpeming, a small town in the state's upper peninsula, had a 25–1 record, but it was no match for Country Day. Webber totaled 25 points and 16 rebounds to lead the Yellowjackets to an 82–43 victory.

For the 1989–90 season, Country Day played in Class B. The school had not gained enough new students to qualify for Class A, but Keener wanted his team to have tougher competition. Webber and his teammates cruised to a 70–50 win over Grand Rapids Northview in the semifinals.

The championship game at the Palace of Auburn Hills, home of the Detroit Pistons, should have been a challenge. After all, Country Day's opponent was Saginaw Buena Vista, the previous year's champ which had a 21–4 record for 1989–90. Webber, who by then was six feet eight inches, was on fire in the second half, scoring twenty-three points on five of seven shots from the floor and thirteen of fourteen free throws. He finished the game with 30 points and made his last thirteen straight free throws. The Yellowjackets won their second state title in a row, 59–53.

For Webber's senior year, Keener scheduled

Webber knows that it is important to be a good free throw shooter. Once, during a state championship game, he made thirteen free throws in a row.

games all over Michigan, against some of the state's toughest schools. He wanted to give lots of fans a chance to see his superstar. By then, Chris had been an All-Stater for three years and was almost a sure bet to make it again as a senior. He was attracting attention from reporters and college coaches from all over the country.

Battle Creek was one of Country Day's stops in January 1991. The Bearcats from Battle Creek Central were 11–0 and the No. 2 ranked team in the Associated Press Class A listings. The Yellowjackets, 10–2, were No. 1 in Class B. In the USA Today poll, they were ranked the 23rd best team in the nation. All 5,800 tickets for the Battle Creek game sold out in a day. Three college coaches were there to watch, too—Michigan's Steve Fisher, Michigan State's Jud Heathcote, and Iowa's Tom Davis. They all wanted Webber to know they wanted him to play basketball for them after his high school graduation.

Chuck Turner, the Battle Creek coach, wasn't interested in Webber's college plans. He wanted his Bearcats to beat Country Day. The way to do that, he figured, was to keep Webber away from the basket. He had his team apply full-court pressure, forcing Chris to stay at midcourt. As Mark Crawford, a Battle Creek television broadcaster, noted, "If Chris Webber gets the ball within four feet of the basket, he will either score or be fouled. You can bet on that."[4]

With the college coaches watching intently and the fans oohing and aahing, Turner's strategy almost worked. Webber only got 18 points, his lowest total of the season, but he managed to get inside for 4 dunks, which brought the crowd to its feet, and directed the ball to his teammates, who managed to score enough points to nip Battle Creek, 62–58.

Some of the Bearcats didn't even seem to mind losing to a superstar. "This is like an exhibition game," said Jo-Jo Boggan. "It's fun playing the number one player in the country."[5] Webber was polite, but he didn't try to make reporters think the game was a big deal. "This was an average crowd for us," he said. "We've played in more hostile arenas."[6]

The fans knew Webber would soon be a player in much bigger arenas. "When Chris Webber makes it big, we'll be able to say we saw him when," wrote Mark Bradley, a columnist for the *Battle Creek Enquirer*.[7]

As expected, the Yellowjackets, by then 24–2, earned a spot in the Class B finals at the Palace in March. Despite their undefeated record, the Albion Wildcats, their opponents, knew they would have their hands full. "Ever since I was a sophomore," said Albion's David Washington, "it's been Chris Webber this and Chris Webber that."[8]

Disaster almost struck in the first minute of play. "I was trying to block [Washington's] shot, and in doing so I came down on Iyapo's [Montgomery] foot," Chris said.[9] Webber fell to the floor with a twisted ankle, and the crowd fell silent. Was the country's top high school basketball talent going to have to watch the rest of his final game from the bench? "This is a great time for this to happen," he told himself.[10]

For most of the rest of the opening quarter, Webber sat on the bench while the team trainer worked on his ankle. With three minutes and nine seconds left, he was back on the floor. His first shot was a slam dunk that gave Country Day its first lead, 10–9. The Wildcats were in trouble because, as Chris said later, "I always seem to play better when I'm hurt."[11]

Country Day led for most of the rest of the way, sometimes by as many as eight points. Late in the third quarter, however, Albion battled back when a Washington slam dunk narrowed the margin to 37–35. Webber came back with a dunk of his own.

Albion's Damon Lewis popped in a jumper, but Webber answered with another bucket. After a pair of Montgomery free throws and two by Webber,

Country Day had a more comfortable 45–37 lead. After that, the Wildcats never came closer than four. The final score was 68–57.

Coach Keener was asked about winning three straight state titles. "This year it's a different feeling," he said. "I have a warm, fuzzy feeling inside."[12] The biggest reason for his warm, fuzzy feeling, though, was done playing for Country Day.

For four years, the Webber family had been contacted by coaches and fans from the country's major colleges. Almost all of them wanted Chris on their teams. Only Dean Smith of North Carolina told him he would be happier playing somewhere else. At first, Webber had planned on attending Michigan State, just like his hero Magic Johnson.

Then, in February of his senior year, he watched a Michigan game at Crisler Arena with his friend Jalen Rose. It didn't take long for them to be spotted by the Wolverine fans. Soon the crowd was cheering for them. After Michigan lost to Purdue, Coach Fisher told them his team needed them for the next season. Chris and Jalen couldn't help smiling.

In the spring, Webber heard that Juwan Howard and Jimmy King, two other great high school stars, had decided to sign with Michigan. He and Rose thought it would be great if they could all play

FACT

Two NBA superstars, Magic Johnson and Larry Bird, first faced each other in the championship game of the 1979 NCAA postseason tournament. Johnson's Michigan State Spartans defeated Bird's Indiana State Sycamores, 75–64.

Breaking toward the basket, Webber looks to make a big play. After his senior season, Parade *magazine named him the nation's top high school player.*

together. Maybe they could help Michigan win a national championship.

After the state championship victory over Albion, Webber and the rest of the Yellowjackets celebrated at a Detroit restaurant. When the meal was over, he told waiting reporters he had decided to go to Michigan.

After putting on a Wolverine cap, Chris listened to the cheers of his teammates, then explained, "I don't want to be a dumb athlete. Today in America, and being black, you need everything you can get. I need a good education."

How did he think he'd do at Michigan? "I think I'm one of the best. I don't know if I can say I'm the best."[13]

Steve Fisher didn't have any doubt. Webber had just won the state's Mr. Basketball award, and *Parade* magazine had named him the nation's top high school player. Michigan's coach looked forward to working with Chris and the other freshmen, whose motto would soon be "Shock the world!"

Chapter 4

Wolverines

Chris Webber and his pal from Detroit, Jalen Rose, were together at the same school, the University of Michigan. They were roommates in South Quad, the dormitory where the other freshman basketball players, Juwan Howard, Jimmy King, and Ray Jackson, also lived.

Howard was a six-foot-ten-inch forward from Chicago. King, a six-foot-four-inch guard, and Jackson, a six-foot-five-inch guard, were both from Texas. Other coaches were amazed at the talent Coach Steve Fisher had recruited. Almost right away, sportswriters dubbed them The Fab Five. Wolverine fans hoped the freshmen would guarantee them four years of powerhouse basketball.

Early in the fall of 1991, even before regular practices had begun, the Fab Five gathered for practice games with the sophomores, juniors, and seniors who were also on the team. It didn't take long for tempers to flare. Chris Seter, a senior, reminded King that he and his friends were just freshmen.

The Fab Five didn't like to be pushed around—and they stuck together. Rose challenged the upperclassmen to a game against the freshmen. He figured it was time to show the veteran players what he and his friends could do.

On one of the first plays, Rose flipped an alley-oop pass to Webber, who slammed it through the hoop. Then the rest of them took turns dunking the ball. Even when they weren't shooting, they looked sharp, racing all over the court. Fast breaks. Rebounds. Steals. The upperclassmen felt like they were standing still. After a while, it seemed like they were being given a lesson.

Not only were they whipping "the big boys," the Fab Five were whooping and hollering all the way. After a good play, they yelled and smiled and point-ed to each other. High fives all around. Trash talking and taunts. It didn't take the freshmen long to decide that they were going to enjoy playing basketball at Michigan. They couldn't wait for the season to begin.

U of M's first game of the 1991 season came on December 2, at Cobo Arena in downtown Detroit.

FACT

Ann Arbor is the home of the University of Michigan Wolverines. It is located only about fifty miles west of Detroit. In about an hour, the Webber family could drive from their home to Crisler Arena, where the Wolverines play their home games. Michigan Stadium, home of the football team, is also a popular destination for sports fans. The stadium can hold up to 105,000 spectators.

Webber, Rose, and Howard were in the starting lineup against the University of Detroit-Mercy Titans.

The first three times he touched the ball, Howard threw it away twice and traveled. Fisher put him on the bench. The rest of the team didn't do much better. Before the night was over, the Wolverines committed 34 turnovers. Of course, they had a few good plays, too. The most impressive one was Rose's alley-oop, which Chris converted into a vicious dunk.

Fortunately, Detroit was a slower, shorter team, and Michigan was able to win easily, 100–74, but Fisher knew his men would have to do much better

Chris Webber patiently waits to re-enter the game. Webber was not on the sidelines much during his time at the University of Michigan. He started every game.

against the nation's top teams. Webber finished with 19 points and 17 rebounds, but he also fouled out and committed 7 turnovers.

The first serious challenge to the Wolverines came in the fifth game of the season, when they faced Duke, the defending national champions, on national television.

Early in the game, Chris went up and over Christian Laettner, the Blue Devils' superstar center, for a slam dunk. "You're weak!" he taunted. "You ain't nothing!"

Laettner wasn't impressed. "Go away, little schoolboy!" he answered.[1]

The Michigan crowd loved it. They could already smell an upset. Soon, however, the first half turned into a disaster. Howard kept traveling. Rose kept fouling. Duke kept scoring. Shortly before intermission, the Blue Devils were ahead by seventeen points. The Michigan fans, blaming their team's problems on the officials, threw trash onto the court.

By halftime, Michigan had narrowed the deficit to 43–33. In the second half, as the Blue Devils began missing shots and turning the ball over, the Wolverines got hot. Webber had three quick dunks. On the way downcourt after the last one, he glared at Laettner. The "schoolboy" was still trying to intimidate the superstar. Now the Michigan fans were on their feet—and this time they weren't throwing garbage.

Then Chris found himself with the ball at the top of the key. The shot clock was running out and all his teammates were covered. What would he do, the fans wondered. Could he handle the pressure?

No problem. Webber calmly went up in the air for a three-pointer. It was good! Now the cheers were almost deafening.

With less than a minute to go, U of M held a 74–71 edge over the defending national champions. Then Rose and Laettner each grabbed a loose ball. "Give it up, little fella," the Blue Devil told the freshman. Rose was furious, but Laettner was laughing at him.[2]

The teams traded free throws, and the Wolverines still led, 76–73, when Laettner tried a three-pointer. Boink! It bounced off the rim. Bobby Hurley grabbed the rebound and went up for another three-point attempt. It looked like Duke's last chance.

Webber raced over to block the shot, but Hurley was able to put it up. The ball bounced off the rim—just as Chris plowed into the Blue Devil, knocking him to the floor. Foul!

Hurley would get three free throws. Each one went up and in. Tie game, 76–76. Just before the buzzer sounded, Webber released a desperation shot from sixty feet out. It headed straight for the basket.

What a finish it was going to be! The ball hit the front of the rim, though, and the game went into overtime.

Webber then tried to get the Wolverines rolling again by poking the ball away from Laettner. A whistle blew, and he had his fifth foul. He had to sit on the bench as the Blue Devils then rolled to an 88–85 victory.

As Laettner and his teammates walked off the floor, they knew how lucky they had been to beat U of M. A Michigan band member held his finger a fraction of an inch from his thumb and yelled, "That much, Christian! That much!"[3]

On February 5, King joined Webber, Rose, and Howard in the starting lineup as the Wolverines buried Northwestern. Four days later, Jackson was a starter, too. Finally, the Fab Five were the starting five.

The game went a lot like the first practice against the upperclassmen in the fall. The freshmen blew by Notre Dame, whipping the ball around the court and into the basket. Once again they whooped and slapped hands, obviously enjoying every minute. They combined to score every one of Michigan's points in a 74–65 win.

It was obvious to basketball fans that the Fab Five had a good deal of talent and attitude—in fact, maybe too much attitude. Many people thought the freshmen spent too much time showing off and showing up their opponents. Why couldn't they just shut up and play basketball?

Late in their first season, they met a legendary athlete whose talent and attitude had made him one of the most famous men in the world, years before they had been born. They bumped into Muhammad Ali, the former heavyweight boxing champion, at a motel in Atlanta, Georgia. He invited them to his room to show them card tricks. Before they left, he gave them three words of advice. "Shock the world!"[4] Now the Fab Five had a motto to go with their talent and attitude.

Of course, they also had style. Before the season had even begun, Brian Dutcher, one of the Wolverines' assistant coaches, noticed that a new look was appearing on basketball players in playgrounds and gyms around the country. Many of the youngsters were wearing long, baggy shorts low on their hips. The outfits looked silly to most adults, but Dutcher knew his team would love them. He added four inches to the length of the Michigan shorts, and the Wolverines had a new look.

Shortly after they met Ali, Webber had a dream that his hair was gone and that he was playing great basketball. It was worth a try, he figured, so he asked Rose to help him shave his head. Then he helped Rose shave his.

When the regular season ended, Michigan had a

One of the things that the Fab Five is remembered for is their long, baggy shorts. They made popular a trend that has now carried over to the NBA.

20–8 record, good enough for a No. 14 ranking. In the postseason NCAA tournament, the Wolverines weren't expected to be a factor. Most experts felt that teams like Kansas, Ohio State, Duke, or the University of California at Los Angeles (UCLA) would be the class of the tournament. They didn't expect Michigan's freshmen to have the experience or the maturity to win against big-time competition.

In the first round, U of M slipped by the Temple Owls, 73–66. Then, with Webber hitting on twelve of fifteen shots from the floor, the Wolverines dropped East Tennessee State, 102–90. When he and Howard had foul trouble against Oklahoma State, senior Eric Riley came off the bench, totaling 15 points and 10 rebounds, to lead Michigan to a thrilling 75–72 victory.

Then they came up against the Ohio State Buckeyes, a team that had already beaten them twice. Just before the opening tip-off, Chris wrapped his arms around the rest of the Fab Five and hugged them. Then he went to work. When Chris Jent went up for a jumper, Webber leaped even higher and slapped the ball away.

It was a wild game, with the lead bouncing back and forth all the way. Finally, with time running out and the score tied, 63–63, Jent let loose a high shot that nobody could touch. Clang! It bounced up, and Chris slapped it away.

FACT

Webber was the first freshman ever to lead the Big Ten Conference in rebounding (9.8 per game). That same season (1991–92), he also was the conference leader in steals (54).

Were the Fab Five nervous going into overtime against one of the toughest teams in the country? Hardly. On the way out for the jump ball, Chris snuck up to Rose and kissed him on the cheek. They both laughed.

Then the Wolverine baskets started falling in. Jumpers. Dunks. Three-pointers. Free throws. Almost immediately, the Buckeyes were down, 72–67. When the buzzer rang, it was 75–71. "We're gonna shock the world!" Howard screamed at the crowd. "Do you believe us now?"[5]

The Fab Five didn't look so sharp in the semifinal game against Cincinnati. Their turnovers helped keep the Bearcats in the game. Then Fisher brought James Voskuil off the bench, and he saved the day with a pair of critical three-pointers late in the game. Michigan won, 76–72.

The title game against Duke was billed as a David-versus-Goliath battle. The Wolverines were the youngsters facing the tough, experienced Blue Devils.

In the first minutes of play, experience didn't count for much as Laettner dribbled the ball off his leg and committed three other turnovers. Soon he was riding the bench. Webber exploded with a one-handed dunk. "Ahhh!" he screamed, as he made a nasty face at the Blue Devils.

Moments later he picked the ball up out of a

FACT

In just five seasons, from 1988 to 1992, Coach Mike Krzyzewski took four Duke teams to the semifinals of the NCAA postseason tournament. The Duke University Blue Devils were whipped by the University of Nevada at Las Vegas (UNLV) in the 1990 title game, 103–73. The next year the Blue Devils became national champions by beating Kansas, 72–65.

tangle of players and shot downcourt, dribbling toward the basket. There he saw Rob Pelinka standing by himself, so he bounced him the ball, flipping it behind his own back right into his teammate's hands. Pelinka tossed in a hook shot, and the Michigan fans went wild.

By halftime, Laettner had 7 turnovers and Michigan had a 31–30 lead. Coach Mike Krzyzewski scolded his players in the locker room. Had they come this far to be embarrassed by a bunch of freshmen?

The second half was an entirely different story. Duke tightened its defense, forcing Michigan to shoot from the outside. The Wolverines started to miss just as Duke began drawing fouls. All of a sudden the Blue Devils had a twenty-point lead. Webber and his teammates couldn't believe it. Late in the game, he slumped on the bench, crying into a towel.

When it was over, Duke had shocked Michigan, 71–51, to win their second consecutive NCAA title. "This is the greatest year I've ever had as a coach," said Krzyzewski.[6]

The Wolverines weren't celebrating, of course. As he left the court, Webber screamed at a television cameraman and tried to get into the locker room quickly. He didn't want the whole country to see him crying.

"I wanted to fight back the tears," he said later. "I really tried, I really did. But I'm human. I hurt. I

Attacking the rim, Webber crushes down a one-handed slam. During the 1992 NCAA Championship Game, Webber put the Wolverines ahead with an early slam, but Duke came back to win the title.

didn't want to do it, but I couldn't stop myself. I didn't want to wait for something I've been dreaming about ever since I was six years old in the backyard playing one-on-one with my father. The dream was right there."[7]

That night Chris Webber was just a nineteen-year-old freshman. There would be many more chances for basketball glory, but he and the Fab Five would have only one more shot at his dream of a national championship.

STATS

1992 NCAA All-Tournament Team

PLAYER	SCHOOL	POSITION
Chris Webber	Michigan	Forward
Jalen Rose	Michigan	Guard
Bobby Hurley	Duke	Guard
Christian Laettner	Duke	Center
Grant Hill	Duke	Forward

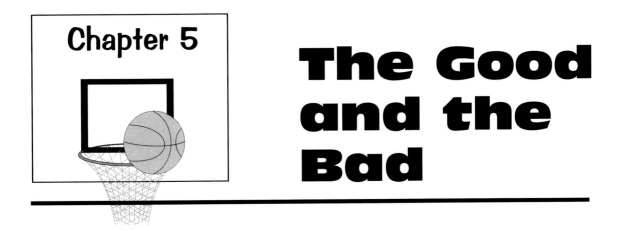

Chapter 5

The Good and the Bad

Nobody ever said the Fab Five weren't confident. As the 1992–93 season began, they had their sights set on the national championship. Chris Webber told reporters the Wolverines would finish the season undefeated.

In their first game, they hardly looked like champions as a weak Rice team led them by six points in the second half. Finally, with Webber netting 20 points and grabbing 19 rebounds, Michigan won, 75–71.

Soon the Wolverines were facing Duke, the squad that had whipped them in the 1992 NCAA final. It was still a strong team. Christian Laettner was the only starter who wasn't back; he had signed a big contract to play in the National Basketball Association (NBA). Webber was asked if he was glad Laettner was gone. "No," he answered. "I wish he was back so we could beat him, too."[1]

Wrong answer. The Blue Devils were infuriated, and they whipped the Wolverines, 79–68.

The Wolverines had better luck at the Rainbow Classic tournament in Hawaii. By beating Nebraska and Kansas, they earned a spot in the title game against North Carolina. Late in that one, Jalen Rose dove for a loose ball, grabbed it, and heaved a soaring pass toward the backboard. Chris caught it and stuffed it, putting Michigan ahead, 77–76.

Derrick Phelps hit a basket to give the Tar Heels a 78–77 lead. With eleven seconds to go, the Wolverines got the ball. Time was almost gone when Jimmy King put up a shot that was supposed to win the game. It missed!

Then there was Jalen Rose, right where he belonged—under the basket, waiting for the rebound. He jumped high, seized the ball, and bounced it off the backboard and through the hoop, just as the buzzer went off. Michigan won, 79–78!

After being named the tournament's most valuable player, Chris was asked if he was going to change his style. He said he'd tried that, and it wasn't any fun. "Earlier this season we were thinking, we're older now, we're sophomores, so let's be really serious and businesslike on the court. I think now

Concentrating on the task at hand, Webber prepares to attempt a free throw. As a Michigan sophomore, Chris was named the most valuable player of the Rainbow Classic tournament.

we're back to being more ourselves, not holding our emotions back."[2]

Chris didn't have any fun at practice a few weeks later, when Eric Riley accidentally elbowed him in the face, breaking his nose. The next day a surgeon repaired the nose, and the day after that, wearing a plastic face mask, Webber started against Minnesota. He scored 12 points and blocked 7 shots, his best ever, as Michigan won, 80–73.

Many reporters and fans thought Chris and Ray Jackson had too much fun after the Wolverines beat Michigan State, 73–69. The two sophomores jumped on the scorers' table and did a victory dance. Of course, many of them still didn't like the team's trash talking, baggy shorts, and bald heads. For their sophomore year, the Fab Five added another fashion statement—black socks. Without telling Coach Steve Fisher or their teammates, they just showed up wearing them at a game. Now the dark socks were part of the "Fab Five look."

Kurt Keener, Webber's high school coach at Country Day, defended him. The attitude was part of his game, he said, and it didn't hurt anybody. "It helps him get into the game emotionally. When he walks onto the court, he kind of goes through a Dr. Jekyll/Mr. Hyde-type thing to do what he feels he has to do to be effective."[3]

Chris wasn't sure why his attitude bothered anybody. "I wink at my players and make faces at the crowd. I'm a very emotional person. I just have to have freedom to express myself on the court after a good play because it keeps me going."[4]

Webber didn't want fans to think he was a jerk. "People automatically assume that the way I am on the court, grimacing and talking trash and all that, is the way I am off the court."[5] That was just the way he and the other Fab Fivers acted when they were playing basketball. "You might look at our bald heads and black shoes and black socks. You might see us very demonstrative on the court. You may say, 'What are they doing?' But every member of the Fab Five is very quiet. We have two different personalities on and off the court."[6]

Keener agreed. "Chris off the court is a fairly quiet kid, very religious. He's a very sophisticated, articulate young man."[7]

The Fab Five might have been stirring up a lot of controversy, but they were incredibly popular with young fans, who loved their style and their attitude. The University of Michigan made millions of dollars selling basketball shorts and jerseys, but Webber and his teammates didn't get a dime of that money. Besides paying the players' tuition and room and board, the school didn't have to give them anything.

While on the court, Chris Webber plays with a lot of emotion. Off the court he is said to be quiet and very religious.

That didn't seem fair to Chris. His family wasn't wealthy, and they couldn't afford to send him a lot of money. "There were times that I didn't have enough money to get a pizza," he said. "A pizza! We made so much money for the school."[8] Of course, he knew the Webbers' financial situation would change drastically when he was finished at Michigan and ready for the NBA. As soon as he became a pro, he would be a millionaire.

As the Wolverines went into the postseason NCAA tournament, they tried to forget about money and about the other controversies that swirled around them. Their regular season record was 26–4, earning them a number five ranking in the polls. Now all they wanted to worry about was the national championship.

It had been a year since the awful loss to Duke in the 1992 title game. "It seemed like the world was going to fall on our shoulders," Rose said about that game.[9] Chris hadn't forgotten, either. "The feeling of last year has been with me for 365 days."[10]

In the opening round, the Wolverines destroyed Coastal Carolina, 84–53, but that would be their last easy win in the tournament. They were supposed to run over UCLA, but the Bruins had other ideas. They surprised Michigan by storming out to a nine-teen-point lead late in the first half, 52–33.

FACT

Chris Webber majored in psychology while at the University of Michigan. If he hadn't become a professional basketball player, he figures he would have become an English teacher.

Then the Wolverines finally went to work, going on a 27–10 tear paced by Webber's three dunks, and finally it was a close game. When regulation time ended, it was tied, 77–77. With 9.4 seconds to go in overtime, it was still 84–84.

Webber threw the ball in to Jalen Rose, who charged the basket and fired up a bank shot that bounced off the rim. Jimmy King flew up to tap the rebound off the board and through the hoop. Michigan won, 86–84!

Against the George Washington Colonials, the much-favored Wolverines only had a 35–33 halftime lead. Each of the Fab Five scored in double figures, and they finally won, 72–64, but they realized it was a poor performance. "We know we haven't played good basketball," Webber said. "We didn't look like Michigan; we looked like a bunch of junior high kids."[11]

In the quarterfinals, the Wolverines went into the locker room at halftime trailing Temple, 35–27. Fisher was angry; his team looked tired and sloppy. "What's the matter with you?" he screamed at Chris. "You're playing like you're in high school!"[12]

Their coach's tirade seemed to wake up Webber and the rest of the team. They took control, outscoring the Owls 23–9 in the opening minutes of the second half and then leading the rest of the way. The final score was 77–72.

Michigan was very lucky to be in the Final Four with Kentucky, North Carolina, and Kansas. They had played poorly throughout the tournament, but squeaked through with a few clutch plays and a lot of luck. Many reporters felt their luck would run out in the semifinal game. "We'll be underdogs against Kentucky," Webber said, "and I say fine, that's as it should be. Nobody thought we'd get to the championship game last year. So what's new?"[13]

He was cooking in the first half against the Wildcats, getting 16 points and 9 rebounds as Michigan went ahead, 40–35. The Wolverines led until Kentucky tied it, 54–54. The lead changed hands nine times before the second half ended with the score still tied, 71–71.

The Wildcats got the first basket in overtime and led until layups by Jackson and Webber put Michigan ahead, 79–78, with forty-one seconds remaining. After Jamal Mashburn missed a free throw, Rose sunk a pair, expanding the lead to 81–78.

Finally, Kentucky had the ball out-of-bounds with four seconds left. Rodney Dent tried to throw it in, but Chris slapped it back at him. When Dent tried again, Chris tipped the ball, caught it, then tossed it in the air. Time had expired, and Michigan was back in the title game!

After coming from behind to win so many games, the Wolverines felt confident they could take North Carolina in the final. They still remembered their thrilling victory in the Rainbow Classic that winter against the Tar Heels.

They were sharp in the opening minutes, going ahead, 23–13, but by halftime North Carolina led, 42–36. The lead switched back and forth in the exciting second half, until Webber got a technical foul for calling a time-out Michigan did not have.

If Chris had not signaled for a T, the Wolverines would have had the ball and a chance to tie the game. Because of his mistake, the Tar Heels got two free throws and possession of the ball with just eleven seconds left.

It was a horrible way for the game to end, even worse than the twenty-point loss to Duke the year before. Webber was very upset, because he felt he had cost his team the national championship they had all wanted so badly. After the game he hugged his dad and cried.

Some fans made fun of Chris for his mistake, but he tried to ignore them. "Anyone who takes that much pleasure in someone else's misfortune has a much bigger problem than I do," he said.[14]

FACT

Michael Jordan's clutch jump shot, with just seventeen seconds left, gave North Carolina a 63–62 victory over Patrick Ewing and Georgetown in the 1982 NCAA title game. It was the Tar Heels' first championship since 1957.

Looking over the situation, Webber searches for an open teammate. His sophomore season at Michigan came to a disappointing end when the Wolverines lost a heartbreaking game to North Carolina.

Most people felt bad for Chris. Isiah Thomas, the Piston star, called to encourage him. Magic Johnson, his old hero, asked if he wanted to practice together during the summer. Even President Bill Clinton sent him a letter. When he appeared at an awards luncheon two days after the game, he was given a standing ovation.

"It's funny," Chris said, "but that time-out incident really helped my popularity. People saw a human side of me in a situation that caused me to weep."[15]

Coach Fisher and the rest of the team reminded fans not to judge Webber's entire college basketball career on the basis of one mistake. For two years the Wolverines had been the most exciting team in the country. "I'll always remember the Fab Five doing what no one thought they could do," said Rose. "And I'll remember Chris Webber making it all possible."[16]

Chapter 6

Webber Goes Pro

It had been an incredible two seasons at the University of Michigan for Chris Webber and the Fab Five. They were the most publicized and controversial college team in the nation. More than that, they had taken the Wolverines to two straight national championship games. When the 1992–93 season ended, they were still just sophomores. That meant that the team could stay together for two more years and two more tries at a national title.

Nobody knew if the team would last that long, though. The Fab Five were not obligated to stay at the University of Michigan. They did not have to finish their junior and senior years. In previous years, some of the nation's best players had left college to try their chances in the National Basketball Association. Magic Johnson had left Michigan State following his sophomore season when the Spartans had taken the 1979 NCAA tournament. Isiah Thomas, Webber's friend from the Detroit Pistons, had done the same thing two years after helping Indiana win the championship. Michael Jordan had left North Carolina a year after the Tar Heels' 1982 triumph.

Why would anybody give up a spot on a great college team? The answer was simple: money. While Webber sometimes had trouble coming up with enough cash to buy a pizza in Ann Arbor, Jordan was earning more than $30 million a year from endorsements and his contract with the Chicago Bulls.

Because he was the Fab Fiver with the best statistics, most attention focused on Webber. Was he ready to play in the NBA? Just two days after the loss to North Carolina, Chris told reporters, "Definitely, I can play now in the NBA. Physically, I'm ready. Mentally, I don't know, and that's where everyone has to make a decision."[1]

Did he really want to quit the team? After all, he had become nationally known at the University of Michigan. The Wolverines, with another year of experience, would be even tougher in 1993–94. "It would be difficult for me to leave," Webber said. "I know some people would find that hard to believe."[2]

Just the day after he called his fatal time-out,

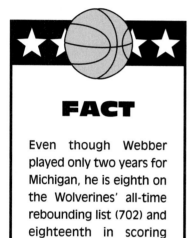

FACT

Even though Webber played only two years for Michigan, he is eighth on the Wolverines' all-time rebounding list (702) and eighteenth in scoring (1,218). He's also second in blocked shots (175).

thousands of fans greeted him and the rest of the Wolverines when they returned to Crisler Arena. Many of them held signs begging him to stay at the school for his junior season. Chris looked quiet and sad when he first entered the arena, but as the cheers and chants grew louder, he couldn't help smiling. "It would be great to stand in front of all these people after winning a championship," he said.[3]

He had to make his decision quickly. After the college season ended, he had less than a month to announce whether he wanted to turn pro and become eligible for the NBA draft. Webber asked NBA stars like Johnson, Thomas, Joe Dumars, and Shaquille O'Neal for their advice. All of them told him he should leave college. O'Neal said he was having a lot of fun as a pro. After all, he had signed a six-year contract with the Orlando Magic that would pay him $40 million.

On May 5, Chris announced that he was leaving Michigan for the NBA. He admitted that money played a big part in his decision, but there were other factors, too: "I've been poor all my life. I could wait another year. I'll always be OK even without basketball. I feel I'm mature enough for the next level. I think right now's the certain time for it."

He welcomed the chance to play against the

FACT

During his two years at Michigan, Webber was a starter in all seventy games. He was the first player to be named to the NCAA All-Tournament team in his freshman and sophomore seasons.

STATS

Following are the awards won by Chris Webber during his college career:

YEAR	AWARD
1991–92	NCAA Championship All-Tournament Team
1992–93	NCAA Championship All-Tournament Team
1992–93	NCAA West Regional All-Tournament Team
1992–93	All Big Ten First Team
1992–93	Associated Press First Team All-America
1992–93	Basketball Weekly First Team All-America
1992–93	United Press Inter. First Team All-America
1992–93	USBWA First Team All-America
1992–93	USBWA District IV Team
1992–93	USBWA Player of the Year Finalist
1992–93	Naismith Award Finalist
1992–93	Wooden Award Finalist
1992–93	Michigan's Most Valuable Player Award
1992–93	Michigan's Rebounding Award

superstars of the NBA. His decision, he said, "was necessary for me to keep moving and move on."[4]

Life changed immediately for the Webber family. It looked like Chris would never again have to worry about having enough money to buy pizza. Even before the NBA draft, he signed a contract with a trading card company that would pay him almost a million dollars for the right to put his photograph on basketball cards.

That summer, Webber signed autographs at a national sports card convention in Chicago. Dave Mathis was one of the collectors who showed up early to get one of the promised five hundred places in line. "They opened the door and we ran as hard as we could to get a spot," he said. "You couldn't believe the mad rush. We sprinted. In fact, we knocked a few people down. People tried to buy our spot in line for $150. After I got his autograph, people outside offered me $300 for it."

Why all the fuss for a player who had yet to sign an NBA contract? "Everybody had a feeling he was going to be a superstar," Mathis said. "They knew he was going to be big. I do a lot of card shows and I've never seen anything else like that. This was a Chris Webber frenzy."[5]

As soon as he got the money from the trading card company, Chris bought his father a new car and

FACT

Oakland, California, is the home of the Golden State Warriors. It is also the home of a major-league baseball team, the Athletics, and of a pro football team, the Raiders. Just three miles across the bay from Oakland is San Francisco, home of a major-league baseball team, the Giants, and a pro football team, the 49ers.

his mother a bracelet. Nike, the giant shoe and sports clothing company, invited him to its headquarters in Portland, Oregon. After a meeting with company officials, Chris and his father were given thousands of dollars worth of shoes, sweat suits, and gym bags. Gifts like that are illegal for college athletes, but there's no problem with professionals accepting them.

Before the NBA draft on June 30, pro teams had to decide if they wanted Webber and, if so, how much they were willing to pay him. Mayce Webber took his son on a tour of team offices around the country. When they visited Oakland, California, Golden State Warriors officials were impressed by Chris's size—and his manners. They were surprised when he took off his shirt. "Looked like Hulk Hogan," said Donn Nelson, son of Warriors coach Don Nelson. He certainly looked big enough to play in the NBA. And when Chris talked to his father, he always called him "sir."[6] The Golden State coaches figured that such a respectful young man would be a fine addition to their team.

The Warriors would not have first pick in the 1993 draft though; they were third behind the Orlando Magic and the Philadelphia 76ers. Webber, of course, wasn't the only fine college player up for grabs. Other prospects included Jamal Mashburn, a

Shaquille O'Neal is one of the biggest stars in basketball. Chris Webber thought that he and O'Neal would be teammates when the Orlando Magic drafted Chris with the first pick in the 1993 draft.

six-foot-eight-inch forward from Kentucky, Anfernee Hardaway, a six-foot-seven-inch guard from Memphis State, and Shawn Bradley, a seven-foot-six-inch center from Brigham Young University. All the young athletes hoped they would be chosen early in the draft. The top choices were guaranteed a lot of attention from the press and fans, as well as the biggest contracts.

Webber and his family and all the other top prospects were at the Palace of Auburn Hills, site of the draft. David Stern, commissioner of the NBA, announced the first pick: The Magic wanted Chris.

The Webbers jumped to their feet. Mayce hugged his son and began to cry. Doris gave her boy a kiss on the cheek. Chris's brothers exchanged high fives. What a moment! Of all the available college talent in the country, Chris had been chosen first. Within a few weeks, he would be signing a contract with the Magic for millions of dollars. That fall he would begin playing alongside O'Neal, already one of the NBA's superstars. Together they should make the Magic one of the league's toughest teams. With any luck, they would be fighting for NBA titles for the next decade.

Webber's smile had never been bigger than when he stepped up on the stage and tried on a Magic cap. The future had never looked brighter for him and his family. As he explained later, "I get to say to my parents, 'Do whatever you want to do.'" There would be plenty of money to send his brothers and sisters to college. If his mother wanted to quit teaching and return to college for an advanced degree, she could do that, too. Mr. Webber was free to quit his job at the General Motors factory. Chris was free to tell them, "Take a month off and let me send you to Jamaica."[7]

On draft day Chris Webber was traded from the Orlando Magic to the Golden State Warriors for Anfernee "Penny" Hardaway, and three future first-round draft picks.

Webber didn't wear the Orlando cap for long. While he was celebrating, the Philadelphia 76ers took Shawn Bradley, and the Warriors chose Hardaway. Then the real action began. Orlando and Golden State announced that they had already agreed to switch their choices. Webber would go to the Warriors, and Hardaway would be playing for the Magic. To sweeten the deal, Golden State gave Orlando its first-round draft picks for 1996, 1998, and 2000.

Now Webber switched hats. The Magic had decided that after the big contract they had signed the year before with O'Neal, they didn't have enough money to pay Chris, too. Hardaway would come cheaper, and he'd be an excellent teammate for Shaq. On top of that, they'd also get those three draft choices. The future looked great for Orlando—even without Webber.

FACT

Rick Barry's 36 points in Game 2 of the 1975 NBA Finals helped overcome the Washington Bullets' thirteen-point lead and gave the Golden State Warriors a 92–91 victory. The Warriors eventually took the title in a four-game sweep as Barry was named MVP. It was the Warriors' last league championship.

So what was in it for Golden State? "Our time is now!" Don Nelson yelled to a crowd of 4,500 in Oakland. They were all sure that Chris would make the Warriors one of the NBA's most powerful teams. Chris Mullin, Golden State's veteran forward, had practiced against Webber to prepare for the 1992 Olympics as part of the United States Dream Team, probably the greatest collection of basketball talent ever assembled. He told his coach how impressed the superstars had been. "When the Dream Team took their showers," Nelson said, "they were only talking about one guy—Webber. He has the best hands I've ever seen. This guy catches everything."[8]

When he put on the Warriors cap, Chris tried not to sound disappointed. "This is still a great thrill, to be the No. 1 player taken. It tells me teams are trying to find what they need. Maybe I wasn't the right thing for Orlando. I thought about everything, from playing for Orlando to playing for Alaska. But I like Golden State's style of offense. It's going to work out the best for me. I'm just glad I was chosen No. 1."[9]

Hardaway, however, seemed even happier. "Not to knock Golden State, but I'm going to love playing with Shaquille O'Neal."[10]

Webber's representatives and the Warrior management began to negotiate a contract. It was a

After signing a fifteen-year $74 million contract with the Golden State Warriors, Webber was all smiles.

tedious process that lasted throughout the summer. Chris spent his time staying in shape. "I ran every day, lost twenty pounds. I played at 265 pounds last year and I'm down to 245 now. I worked a lot on my post game, things they asked me to do. I ran with [Joe] Dumars and Isiah [Thomas] a couple of times, played with them a lot."[11]

The contract negotiations dragged on as the season approached. Then, on October 6, Webber was rushed into surgery for an appendectomy. Would the operation affect his career? The Warriors weren't worried. Twelve days later they agreed to a fifteen-year, $74 million deal. They were confident he would soon recover.

On October 21, Chris practiced with the team. At first, he had to take it easy because he was still a little sore. Also, he had spent several days on his back recovering in the hospital and at home. "It's hard." he said, "when you're going full tilt against guys who are in shape."[12]

Webber told his teammates he was ready to give his best efforts. He hired a trainer to set up a weight-lifting program to strengthen his upper body even further.

He felt so good about his future in the NBA that he was able to joke about the time-out fiasco in the

NCAA title game. "If Coach Nelson tells me to call a time-out, I pass to Chris Mullin."[13]

Webber insisted that he was ready to do whatever had to be done to make Golden State a contender. "I'm not trying to win individual awards. I just want to fit in and win games for my team. I'll be a good player for them because I'll do what they tell me."[14]

Chapter 7

Rookie Year

Chris Webber recovered from his appendectomy in time to play in the Golden State Warriors' final two preseason games in the fall of 1993. Then he sprained his left ankle and missed the first two regular season games.

Webber wasn't the only Warrior having problems staying healthy. Tim Hardaway, their All-Star guard, tore a knee ligament at an October practice and was lost for the season. Chris Mullin, their superstar forward, ripped a finger ligament and missed the first twenty games of the season.

Webber had hoped to play forward, his position in high school and college, but Coach Don Nelson had other ideas. He decided to move Chris to center. The move didn't make a lot of sense to Chris, but he didn't complain publicly, and he promised to work hard to learn the new position.

In only his third game with Golden State, Webber grabbed 13 rebounds. Three days later, he put a move on Charles Barkley that brought the Oakland crowd to its feet. Getting the ball on a fast break, he raced downcourt, then faked out Sir Charles by spinning the ball around his waist. He finished off the play by going up and over Barkley and delivering a massive slam dunk.

Four days later, he had 18 rebounds in a 112–97 loss to Seattle. On December 23, the Warriors destroyed the Los Angeles Clippers 141–95 as he picked up the first triple double of his pro career— 22 points, 12 rebounds, and 12 assists.

Webber had a great rookie season, and, despite all their injuries, the Warriors compiled a 50–32 record, good enough for the playoffs. He had become the first rookie ever to get more than 1,000 points, 500 rebounds, 250 assists, 150 blocks, and 75 steals. In the fifteen previous years, only three veteran players—Kareem Abdul-Jabbar, Hakeem Olajuwon, and David Robinson—had accomplished that feat.

Chris, the youngest player in the NBA, was honored as the league's rookie of the year. In a 53–47 vote of sports journalists, he beat out Anfernee Hardaway, who was having a fine season with the Orlando Magic.

Coach Nelson told reporters that he was very pleased with his star rookie. "He has the mental and physical capacities to be a great player. And the desire is there. He just has to be the best. It's driven in him. I don't know where it came from, but I love it. He can't miss."[1] He was sure that Chris would continue to improve. "He's the best thing that has happened to this franchise, and to me personally, in the last dozen years."[2]

A year of experience, Webber said, had taught him to take better care of his body. "I can't eat a lot of junk food. But I love potato chips. I always used to eat barbecue chips, and candy and drink pop. I learned that you really can't do that because you don't have as much energy when you eat those types of things."[3]

He said the highlight of the season for him had been his first game on November 9, against the Houston Rockets. "I wish I could say that it was when I dunked on Charles Barkley, because everybody remembers that. But I'd say my first game, because that was when I was the happiest and I realized that playing in the NBA was my dream come true."[4]

It was a very enjoyable season, but Webber couldn't help thinking about his years at Michigan as one of the Fab Five. "You never realize how much fun you have in college until you leave," he said.

"There's more family, more friends. Here it's more of a business."[5]

Even though he had no problems with his Golden State teammates, he occasionally wondered about what would have happened if he had been on the Magic with Shaquille O'Neal. "I think we would have been the game's most devastating front line," he said.

The Warriors didn't last long in the playoffs. Barkley and the Phoenix Suns ended their season with three straight defeats.

By then, rumors had begun to surface that, despite their kind words in public, Chris and Coach Nelson were not getting along. Webber still didn't enjoy playing center, and he resented the fact that he got a lot of bench time in the fourth quarters of close games.

The coach told several players that he didn't think the rookie was improving quickly enough. "Coach told the guards the reason we were losing was Chris Webber," said Billy Owens, Webber's closest friend on the team.[6]

Nelson reportedly once became so infuriated with Chris's playing that he told the rookie, "I can't believe we drafted you No. 1." Then, at a team meeting, he told him, "I love your game. That's why I drafted you No. 1."[7]

FACT

Some of the greatest NBA stars began their pro careers by winning rookie of the year honors:

Wilt Chamberlain	(1960)
Rick Barry	(1966)
Larry Bird	(1980)
Michael Jordan	(1985)
Patrick Ewing	(1986)
David Robinson	(1990)
Shaquille O'Neal	(1993)
Chris Webber	(1994)
Grant Hill	(1995)

His opponents can only stand and watch as Webber delivers a rim-rattling baseline jam. Webber was selected as the Rookie of the Year for the 1993–94 season.

Meanwhile, Mayce Webber was finishing up the last year and a half of his thirty years with General Motors. Why was he still working in a factory when his son was a multimillionaire? "No young kid is going to tell me whether I should work or not," he joked. More seriously, he said, "I want to be an

STATS

Number 1 Draft Picks That Became Rookie of the Year

YEAR	PLAYER	COLLEGE	DRAFT TEAM
1969	Lew Alcindor*	UCLA	Milwaukee Bucks
1983	Ralph Sampson	Virginia	Houston Rockets
1985	Patrick Ewing	Georgetown	New York Knicks
1987	David Robinson	Navy	San Antonio Spurs
1990	Derrick Coleman	Syracuse	New Jersey Nets
1991	Larry Johnson	UNLV	Charlotte Hornets
1992	Shaquille O'Neal	LSU	Orlando Magic
1993	Chris Webber	Michigan	Orlando Magic**
1996	Allen Iverson	Georgetown	Philadelphia 76ers
1997	Tim Duncan	Wake Forest	San Antonio Spurs
1999	Elton Brand***	Duke	Chicago Bulls

*Lew Alcindor changed his name to Kareem Abdul-Jabbar in 1971.
**Chris Webber played his rookie season for the Golden State Warriors.
***Brand was named Co-rookie of the Year with Steve Francis.

example to my children. I want them to know that you have to work hard to earn your money, and that you should complete what you start."[8]

Chris said he had learned another lesson about work from his father. Coach Nelson "didn't treat me with respect. And my father had taught me, don't ever have a job you don't love."[9]

Nelson was tired of the troubles with Webber. "All of a sudden I can't coach anymore," he said, "when all I've done is reprimand a couple of young players who challenged my authority."[10]

Webber didn't want the problem to continue, either. Late in March he said, "Things are going to happen in the off-season. Something has to happen."[11]

Still, nothing happened. When practices began for the 1994–95 season, the Warriors were still torn by the bad feeling between their head coach and his star player. Then Nelson traded Owens to Miami. "When they got rid of me," Owens said, "Web told me he was not going to play there [for Golden State]."[12]

By then, Nelson and Webber weren't even speaking to each other. If they couldn't patch up their differences quickly, one of them would have to go.

Chapter 8

A New Start in Washington

Chris Webber was very serious about wanting to get away from Golden State Coach Don Nelson. In the off-season, he terminated his $74 million contract with the team. The move was perfectly legal. His lawyers had inserted a clause in the original contract that allowed him to leave the Warriors if he wasn't happy.

It was a risky financial move. Webber was giving up millions just for the right to talk to other teams about joining them. According to the contract, Golden State could still match any offers he received and keep him on the team.

By terminating the contract, Webber was forcing the team to take action. The perfect solution, as far as he was concerned, would be for the team to fire

Nelson. With a new coach, Chris would probably be happy to be a Warrior again. "I rejected that," said Chris Cohan, the team's owner. "I want Don to stay."[1]

Meanwhile his old Fab Five teammate, Juwan Howard, was having contract problems of his own. After his junior year at Michigan, Howard had left the college for the National Basketball Association. In the 1994 draft, he had been selected by the Washington Bullets, but by early November no contract had been signed. The Bullets had a reputation for low salaries, and they couldn't agree on terms with Howard.

Without contracts, Chris and Juwan were on the sidelines as the 1994–95 NBA season began. After missing the first six games, Webber and Golden State finally signed a one-year, $2.3 million contract on November 16. It looked like Chris would soon be taking orders again from Coach Nelson—or would he?

The next day, before he even had a chance to put his uniform back on, Webber was traded to the Bullets. It turned out that the new contract was just a way to get rid of Chris and get something in return. Without it, Golden State couldn't have traded him for Tom Gugliotta and first-round draft picks in 1996, 1998, and 2000.

FACT

Don Nelson is one of the most experienced coaches in the NBA. His first head coaching job was with the Milwaukee Bucks (1976–87). Nelson moved on to the Golden State Warriors in 1988, the New York Knicks in 1996, and the Dallas Mavericks in 1997. He has been named Coach of the Year three times: 1983, 1985, and 1992.

On the same day, the Bullets finally signed Howard to an eleven-year, $36.6 million contract. Not only did Webber have a new team, he would be reunited with his old friend from Michigan. "I want to be here for the rest of my career," he announced.[2]

Jim Lynam, Washington's first-year coach, was thrilled about the additions to his team. "More than anything," he said, "this brings excitement to the team and to the city."[3] Suddenly there was interest in the Bullets, a team that had posted a terrible 24–58 record in 1993–94. More than 1,200 season tickets were sold in the first twenty-four hours after Webber and Howard became Bullets. The fans

Chris Webber celebrates with the fans at a Washington Bullets game. Webber was traded from the Golden State Warriors to the Washington Bullets in 1994.

hoped that their team would now have the same attitude—and success—the two young men had enjoyed at Michigan. As Juwan said, "Losing is contagious and I just can't accept it. Don't want to. Winning is what puts a smile on my face."[4]

By then, Webber had a reputation as an athlete who didn't listen to his coaches. Steve Fisher, some fans figured, hadn't tried to control Chris at Michigan; he just let him do what he wanted. When Nelson tried to tell him what to do at Golden State, Webber rebelled.

The criticism angered Chris. "I look like the spoiled, demanding brat when that's not the case at all."[5] Jalen Rose, his former teammate at Michigan, agreed. "It's not that Chris doesn't want to be yelled at. Chris wants a coach who is going to be hard on him."[6]

Kurt Keener, his coach at Country Day High School, said, "Chris was a lonely kid last season. He'd fly out high school buddies to keep him company. Chris comes from an unusually close-knit family. He probably was looking for a little more interpersonal relationship with the coach."[7]

On the morning of November 19, Webber arrived in Washington after an overnight flight from San Francisco. The Bullets had a game scheduled that night against the Boston Celtics. Lynam asked

Chris if he would be ready to play. After all, there wouldn't even be time for a practice before the game, and he hadn't even met the entire team yet. Susan O'Malley, the team president, said the fans were expecting him. "They are going to burn the house down if you don't play."[8]

Chris was anxious to meet his teammates and get on the court. When he and Howard were introduced to the sellout crowd that night, the fans jumped to their feet and roared. They had hopes that Washington would soon be contending for an NBA championship. Even though he only played twenty-three minutes against the Celtics, Webber had 9 points, 9 rebounds, and 4 blocked shots. Juwan, who had only practiced once with the team, had 10 points and 11 rebounds. The happy Bullets fans didn't even seem to mind that Boston won, 103–102.

They did notice when the team dropped twenty-three of its next twenty-six games. The two Fab Fivers were great additions, but, obviously, the Bullets still had far to go before they would be a power in the league.

When Webber returned to Oakland on December 22, he was not a popular figure. The fans there blamed him for the trouble with Nelson and felt he had abandoned them. The boos were still echoing through the arena in the third quarter, when he went after a loose ball and fell on his left side. He had to leave the game with a dislocated shoulder that kept him out of action for nineteen more games.

After Webber returned to the lineup, he led the Bullets in scoring in five of their next twenty games, and in rebounds in eight. The team won only two of its next thirteen games, though, and he wasn't used to losing. "It's hard when you're losing to enjoy what you are doing," he said. "It just gets to you. I take this job very seriously."[9] On the court, he began

Calling for the ball, Webber waits to receive a pass from teammate Juwan Howard. When Washington traded for Webber these former college teammates were reunited.

to look distracted and tired; it was obvious he wasn't having fun. Since he was a team leader, his sullen attitude didn't help his teammates. "I may have cheated some of the players by not patting them on the back when I may have needed a pat on the back. When you're supposed to be a leader, you need help, too."[10]

Webber soon realized that, win or lose, he had an obligation to give his best every night on the court. Early in March, Bullets fans noticed his big smile was back when he sank a key three-pointer against the New Jersey Nets. He sneered at the Nets when Washington finally won, 110–102. It was only the team's sixteenth victory of the season, but it gave them a taste of what they expected in the future.

Chris finished the season as the team leader in scoring (20.1 points per game), rebounding (9.6), and steals (1.54). The Bullets, of course, didn't make it to the playoffs with their 21–61 record. It was their seventh losing season in a row, but Lynam had hopes that his two former Wolverines would one day turn things around. "Chris Webber and Juwan Howard are undoubtedly the heart of this team," he said. "I envision this powerful pair of young forwards bringing us great depth and exceptional athletic ability."[11]

Abe Pollin, the Bullets' owner, was even more

FACT

Before games, Chris Webber gets pumped up by listening to rap music in the locker room. He relaxes by reading. One of his favorite books is *Great Black Thinkers and Inventors*.

optimistic. On October 8, 1995, when Webber signed a six-year, $58 million deal with the team, he said, "We are going to bring an NBA championship to Washington, and Chris Webber is going to lead the way."[12]

He had his best game of the 1995–96 season when the Bullets beat the Warriors, 115–114, on December 28. Webber's 40 points were a career high. He hit on eighteen of twenty-five shots from the floor, grabbed 10 rebounds, and contributed 10 assists. "I was just in a zone tonight," he said. "I can't take all the credit, though, this was a whole team effort. It just feels good to get that win."[13] Howard added 24 points.

"Both him and Juwan really dominated," said Rick Adelman, the Warriors coach. He [Webber] was hitting them all night."[14] Lynam agreed. "He was sensational tonight."[15]

Webber's season didn't last much longer. After he reinjured his shoulder, surgeons repaired it on February 1, 1996. He had to watch the rest of Washington's disappointing season from the bench.

In 1996–97 the Bullets enjoyed their best season since 1978–79. Webber led the team in both scoring and rebounding, while making his first appearance in the NBA All-Star Game. The Bullets finished, 44–38, and made the playoffs. Though the team

Webber's 1995–96 season was cut extremely short due to injuries. He is expected to be fully recovered for 1996–97, and will try to lead the Bullets into the NBA playoffs.

played well, the Bullets lost to the eventual champion Chicago Bulls in three straight games.

For the start of the 1997–98 season, the Bullets changed names. The team was now known as the Washington Wizards. The Wizards finished with a winning record for the second straight season. The team finished the season with 4 wins in a row. However, they were eliminated from the playoffs on the last day of the season. Webber again led the team in scoring and rebounding.

The 1998–99 season was cut short by a labor dispute, and the teams played just 50 games. Webber was traded by the Wizards to the Sacramento Kings before the season began. He responded by leading the Kings to the playoffs and leading the league with 13.0 rebounds per game. Webber, along with center Vlade Divac, and guard Jason Williams, led Sacramento to the playoffs again in 1999–2000. In both the 1999 and 2000 playoffs the Kings lost in the first round of hard-fought series. Still, their up-tempo style has given them a reputation as one of the most exciting teams in the league.

Chris Webber looks forward to a long, successful career in the NBA. "Ten years from now, I'd like to be regarded in the same breath as Larry Bird, Magic Johnson and Michael Jordan. I don't know if I'll ever get there, but I'm going to try."[16]

Chapter Notes

Chapter 1

1. "NCAA Championship," CBS-TV broadcast, April 5, 1993.

2. Ibid.

3. George Vecsey, "The Man Behind the Glare and the Trash Talk," *The New York Times*, April 5, 1993, p. C6.

4. Ibid.

5. Malcolm Moran, "Stage Is Set: Control vs. Cockiness," *The New York Times*, April 5, 1993, p. C6.

6. Mitch Albom, *Fab Five* (New York: Warner Books, 1993), p. 334.

7. Paul Attner, "Systematic Victory," *The Sporting News*, April 12, 1993, p. 41.

8. Ibid.

9. Alexander Wolff, "Technical Knockout," *Sports Illustrated*, vol. 78, no. 14, April 12, 1993, p. 27.

10. Malcolm Moran, "It's Michigan's Call, but It's Carolina's Title," *The New York Times*, April 6, 1993, p. B15.

11. William F. Reed, "I Cost Our Team the Game," *Sports Illustrated*, vol. 78, no. 14, April 12, 1993, p. 28.

12. "NCAA Championship."

13. Dave Kindred, "One Great Run Ends One Short," *The Sporting News*, April 12, 1993, p. 42.

14. Paul Attner, "The Price of Success," *The Sporting News*, April 12, 1993, p. 40.

15. Tom Friend, "Webber Keeps Word and Luncheon Date," *The New York Times*, April 8, 1993, p. B13.

Chapter 2

1. Tom Povtat, "The Eternal Optimist Sets a Goal: Greatness," *The Sporting News*, July 19, 1993, p. 43.

2. George Vecsey, "The Man Behind the Glare and the Trash Talk," *The New York Times*, April 5, 1993, p. C6.

3. Povtat, p. 43.

4. Billy Sharp, "10 Questions With Chris Webber," *NBA Inside Stuff*, vol. 3, no. 1, January/February 1995, p. 26.

5. Bruce Schoenfeld, "Getting a Read on Chris Webber," *The Sporting News*, January 24, 1994, p. 38.

6. Ibid.

7. Phil Taylor, "Beating the Blues," *Sports Illustrated*, vol. 78, no. 15, April 19, 1993, p. 54.

8. Ibid., p. 54–55.

9. Mitch Albom, *Fab Five* (New York: Warner Books, 1993), p. 54.

10. Schoenfeld, p. 38.

Chapter 3

1. Bruce Schoenfeld, "Getting a Read on Chris Webber," *The Sporting News*, January 24, 1994, p. 38.

2. Ibid., p. 36.

3. Steve Gordon, "Child's Play," *Sport*, vol. 84, no. 4, April 1993, p. 79.

4. "Battle Creek Central vs. Country Day," WUHQ-TV broadcast, January 26, 1991.

5. Mark Bradley, "It Was Really a Big Show," *Battle Creek Enquirer*, January 27, 1991, p. C1.

6. Ibid.

7. Ibid.

8. Bob Reed, "Win or Lose, Albion Now Respected," *Battle Creek Enquirer*, March 23, 1991, p. 1B.

9. Mark Bradley, "Albion Settles For 2nd Place," *Battle Creek Enquirer*, March 24, 1991, p. 3D.

10. Ibid., p. 1D.

11. Ibid.

12. Ibid., p. 3D.

13. Associated Press dispatch from Detroit, March 23, 1991.

Chapter 4

1. Mitch Albom, *Fab Five* (New York: Warner Books, 1993), p. 88.

2. Ibid., p. 90.

3. Curry Kirkpatrick, "Boys to Men," *Sports Illustrated*, vol. 76, no. 13, April 6, 1992, p. 15.

4. Albom, p. 140.

5. Ibid., p. 159.

6. Gannett News Service dispatch from Minneapolis, April 1992.

7. Ibid.

Chapter 5

1. Mitch Albom, *Fab Five* (New York: Warner Books, 1993), p. 221.

2. Phil Taylor, "Paradise Found," *Sports Illustrated*, vol. 78, no. 1, January 11, 1993, p. 56.

3. Steve Gordon, "Child's Play," *Sport*, vol. 84, no. 4, April 1993, p. 79.

4. Ibid.

5. Bruce Schoenfeld, "Getting a Read on Chris Webber," *The Sporting News*, January 24, 1994, p. 37.

6. Dave Kindred, "One Great Run Ends One Short," *The Sporting News*, April 12, 1993, p. 42.

7. Gordon, p. 79.

8. William C. Rhoden, "Transition from East to West," *The New York Times*, February 12, 1994, p. 29.

9. Malcolm Moran, "Stage Is Set: Control vs. Cockiness," *The New York Times*, April 5, 1993, p. C6.

10. Ibid.

11. Alexander Wolff, "A Fearsome Foursome," *Sports Illustrated*, vol. 78, no. 13, April 5, 1993, p. 18.

12. Albom, p. 305.

13. Wolff, p. 18.

14. Phil Taylor, "Beating the Blues," *Sports Illustrated*, vol. 78, no. 15, April 19, 1993, p. 56.

15. Walter Roessing, "Time Out With Chris Webber," *Boys Life*, vol. 84, no. 12, December 1994, p. 18.

16. Kindred, p. 42.

Chapter 6

1. Tom Friend, "Webber Keeps Word and Luncheon Date," *The New York Times*, April 8, 1993, p. B13.

2. Phil Taylor, "Beating the Blues," *Sports Illustrated*, vol. 78, no. 15, April 19, 1993, p. 56.

3. Ibid.

4. Associated Press dispatch from Ann Arbor, May 5, 1993.

5. Interview with Dave Mathis, November 15, 1995.

6. Tom Friend, "Warriors Think Big With Webber in Hand," *The New York Times*, July 1, 1993, p. B13.

7. Ric Bucher, "I'll Do What They Tell Me," *The Sporting News*, November 8, 1993, p. 9.

8. Friend, p. B13.

9. Clifton Brown, "Pick and Troll: Magic Trades No. 1 Choice Webber," *The New York Times*, July 1, 1993, p. B13.

10. Ibid.

11. Bucher, p. 9.

12. Ibid.

13. Walter Roessing, "Time Out With Chris Webber," *Boys Life*, vol. 84, no. 12, December 1994, p. 18.

14. Bucher, p. 9.

Chapter 7

1. Golden State Warriors 1994–95 Media Guide, p. 54.

2. Phil Taylor, "Together Forever," *Sports Illustrated*, vol. 80, no. 5, February 7, 1994, p. 52.

3. Billy Sharp, "10 Questions With Chris Webber," *NBA Inside Stuff*, vol. 3, no. 1, January/February 1995, p. 26.

4. Ibid.

5. William C. Rhoden, "Transition from East to West," *The New York Times*, February 12, 1994, p. 29.

6. Tom Friend, "A Warrior's Continuing Battles," *The New York Times*, December 16, 1994, p. B15.

7. Ibid.

8. Ira Berkow, "The Bullets May Now Be Loaded," *The New York Times*, November 22, 1994, p. B11.

9. Ibid.

10. Phil Taylor, "Not so Golden State," *Sports Illustrated*, vol. 80, no. 12, March 28, 1994, p. 86.

11. Ibid.

12. Friend, p. B15.

Chapter 8

1. Clifton Brown, "Sign Him, Trade Him: Webber Becomes Bullet," *The New York Times*, November 18, 1994, p. B13.

2. David Steele, "Atlantic," Street & Smith's Pro Basketball 1995–96, October 1995, p. 71.

3. Shaun Powell, "Bullets Give Robin Ficker Something to Cheer About," *The Sporting News*, November 28, 1994, p. 42.

4. Steele, p. 71.

5. Harvey Araton, "Webber Finds Way to Escape a Trap," *The New York Times*, November 17, 1994, p. B16.

6. Ibid.

7. Ibid.

8. Phil Taylor, "Capital Gain," *Sports Illustrated*, vol. 81, no. 22, November 28, 1994, p. 18.

9. Frank Hughes, "Webber Starting to Regain Old Fire," *Washington Times*, March 3, 1995, p. B4.

10. Ibid.

11. Jim Lynam, "Washington Bullets," *Street & Smith's Pro Basketball 1995–96*, October 1995, p. 95.

12. Associated Press dispatch from Washington, D.C., October 8, 1995.

13. America Online, December 29, 1995.

14. Ibid.

15. Ibid.

16. Tom Povtat, "The Eternal Optimist Sets a Goal: Greatness," *The Sporting News*, July 19, 1993, P. 43.

Career Statistics

NBA

YEAR	TEAM	GP	FG%	REB	AST	STL	BLK	PTS	AVG
1993–94	Golden State	76	.552	694	272	93	164	1,333	17.5
1994–95	Washington	54	.495	518	256	83	85	1,085	20.1
1995–96	Washington	15	.543	114	75	27	9	356	23.7
1996–97	Washington	72	.518	743	331	122	137	1,445	20.1
1997–98	Washington	71	.482	674	273	111	124	1,555	21.9
1998–99	Sacramento	42	.486	545	173	60	89	839	20.0
1999–00	Sacramento	75	.483	787	345	120	128	1,834	24.5
Totals		405	.503	4,075	1,725	616	736	8,447	20.9

GP=Games Played   **FG%**=Field Goal Percentage   **REB**=Rebounds   **AST**=Assists
STL=Steals   **BLK**=Blocks   **PTS**=Points scored   **AVG**=Scoring Average

Where to Write Chris Webber

Mr. Chris Webber
c/o Sacramento Kings
One Sports Parkway
Sacramento, CA 95834

On the Internet at:
<http://www.nba.com/playerfile/chris_webber.html>
<http://espn.go.com/nba/profiles/profile/1272.html>

Index